Cloud Forest

Written and photographed by Nic Bishop

Contents

Collins

What is a cloud forest?

A cloud forest is a very special type of forest. It grows high in the mountains where the trees are nearly always covered in clouds. Clouds blow through the trees, wetting their leaves and branches, and rain falls almost every day.

These forests are rare because they only grow on the cloudiest mountain ranges. You can see them in different places around the world, in tropical parts of Asia, Africa, Australia and the Americas.

Cloud forests are rich in plants and animals that live nowhere else on Earth.

They also have secrets to tell us. Many cloud forests are so hard to reach that they haven't been explored by scientists. Perhaps three quarters of their plants and animals haven't yet been found.

Only a tiny number of tropical forests are cloud forests.

■ **tropical cloud forests** (2.5%)
□ other tropical forests (97.5%)

This brilliant flower grows in the cloud forest.

A beetle scurries along a branch.

A climb to the cloud forest

Imagine you are going to climb a tropical mountain. At the bottom you will find **rainforest**. It's very warm and damp and some trees grow as tall as 50 metres, higher than an office block!

As you climb higher up the mountain you'll notice that the air gets cooler and the trees are a little shorter.

Then you'll reach a place where clouds brush against the mountain. Blowing mists soak the leaves and branches of the trees with water that trickles and drips to the ground. This place is the cloud forest and it's very different from the rainforest lower down. It's much cooler and always soggy. Cloud forests can get from three to eight metres of water each year.

rainforest

cloud forest

7

In the cloud forest, the tallest trees are only about 30 metres high. There are hundreds of **mosses** and **ferns** which cover everything in a soft, green coat.

If you study the forest closely, you'll find that many of the plants and animals are different from those in the warm rainforest. They need to be able to cope with the cool dampness of the cloud forest.

As you climb further upwards the air becomes even colder and the trees become even smaller.

Near the top of the mountain, the trees may only be four metres tall. Their growth is crooked and stunted by the strong, cool winds that blow almost every day. The twisted branches look spooky, like the legs and arms of strange, green creatures.

That's why this type of cloud forest is called **elfin forest**.

Cloud forest life

There are lots of different plants and animals that live in cloud forests. But nobody knows exactly how many. Some of them can only live in the cloud forests. Some can only live in one particular cloud forest.

You may find plants and animals in the cloud forest on one mountain that are different to the cloud forest on the very next mountain.

*There are only a few hundred mountain gorillas left.
They live in the cloud forests of Africa.*

Plants

Cloud forests are especially rich in mosses and ferns, which like to grow in damp places. In the cloud forest on Mount Kinabalu in Borneo, there are 600 different kinds of fern growing. That's more kinds of fern than grow in the whole of North America!

Cloud forests are the best place to see tree ferns, which can grow up to five metres tall. Plants like these were growing before dinosaurs walked on Earth.

Many cloud forest plants live in an unusual way. They grow on the branches of trees instead of on the ground.

Normally, plants have to live on the ground so their roots can get water from the soil. But cloud forests are so wet that these plants can gather all the water they need from the mist and rain. This means they can live on the trees, where they get more light than on the ground.

Many of the world's orchids grow in cloud forests.

The overlapping leaves of this plant hold a pool of water in the centre which makes a home for small frogs and insects.

12

Mosses, ferns and **orchids** often grow on the trees.
One tree can have as many as 300 different plants
growing on its branches and trunk.

tree kangaroo

Mammals

Fewer large **mammals** live in cloud forests than in rainforests. But some of these mammals are very unusual.

In New Guinea, kangaroos live in trees like monkeys. These tree kangaroos use their long tails to balance just as monkeys do.

The long-nosed echidna lives in New Guinea's mountain forests. This unusual mammal lays eggs and feeds on earthworms.

New animals are still being discovered. Scientists have recently found new kinds of deer, pigs and rabbits living in a cloud forest in Vietnam.

Echidnas probe the ground with their long noses and catch earthworms with their sticky tongues.

Birds

Many birds visit the cloud forest. They fly up from the rainforest to nest or to look for food.

In New Guinea's cloud forests, large flocks of colourful parakeets look for berries and nuts. If you are really lucky you may spot the rare bird of paradise.

Rare dwarf cassowaries live in New Guinea cloud forests. They eat mostly fruit.

Sicklebill birds of paradise use their long beaks to catch insects.

In Central America, the brilliant green and red quetzal birds raise their young in the cloud forest. Hummingbirds and parrots also add flashes of colour. They come to feed on the forest's bright flowers and fruit.

Quetzals of Central America are among the world's most beautiful birds.

Frogs and lizards

Frogs like to live in damp places, so the cloud forest is perfect for them. Most are **nocturnal**, which means they come out at night. They sleep under logs and leaves by day and wake up after sunset to hunt for insects.

Coquis of Puerto Rico have suckers on their toes so that they can climb up tree trunks and across leaves. They are nocturnal, waking up at sunset to catch small insects.

Many lizards, like this mossy gecko from Madagascar,
have green and brown colours that match their
surroundings. They hide by staying very still, and waiting.
Then, when insects crawl by, the lizards snap them up.

Insects

We know very little about cloud forest insects. During the day colourful butterflies may flutter through the trees, but most insects are nocturnal. Some live on the ground, hiding in the wet blanket of ferns, mosses and dead leaves. Others live among the tree plants.

Beautiful blue morpho butterflies can sometimes be seen in the cloud forests of Central America.

It's best to explore the forest
after dark. That's when you can
see all kinds of insects like
stick insects, moths and beetles.

*Cicadas and grasshoppers both
have brown and green colours
to help them hide.*

Cloud forests in danger

Cloud forests are in danger. They are often small compared to other forests so it doesn't take long to cut them down, and once they are gone, they can't grow again in the same way. People have already destroyed cloud forests for timber, to plant crops or to graze cattle.

endangered Hawaiian
cloud forest plants

Hawaii's unusual cloud forest plants have been threatened by pigs, which dig them out of the ground. The pigs don't belong in the cloud forest. They were released by people and now live wild in the forest. Scientists are growing these rare plants in greenhouses. Then they put them back in the forests, which have been fenced to protect them from pigs.

growing rare cloud forest plants in Hawaii

One of the greatest threats to the cloud forest is **climate change**. Scientists believe that some mountain areas are becoming less cloudy and wet. This is difficult for cloud forest plants and animals, which depend on lots of moisture.

In a cloud forest called Monteverde in Costa Rica, about half of the frogs and toads died after a few dry years. Then the snakes and other animals that depended on the frogs and toads for food started to disappear, too.

Golden toads from Monteverde are now thought to be extinct.

the cloud forest in Costa Rica

Scientists believe the world's climate is getting warmer. This is a problem for plants and animals that like to live where it's cool. Some can survive by living higher up in the mountains, where it's cold enough for them.

But what about the cloud forest plants and animals that already live on the mountain tops?

New Guinea harpy eagle

grasshopper

butterfly

People need cloud forests

It's very important to protect cloud forests, not only for the plants and animals that live there, but for everyone.

cloud water

rain water

water collects in rivers and streams

Cloud forests collect water. This water flows in rivers to the **lowlands**, where people use it for drinking or for watering crops. These rivers keep flowing even when it doesn't rain, because cloud forests collect water straight from the clouds.

If cloud forests are cut down, people will have less water.

Water collected from the clouds and rain in the cloud forest flows downhill for people to use in the lowlands.

The cloud forest also stops mountain soil from sliding down to the lowlands. The trees hold it firm with their roots. If the forest is cut down, heavy rains can wash the soil away and flood the lowlands with mud.

These wild strawberries grow in the cloud forest. So do wild avocados, tomatoes, peppers, beans and potatoes.

Cloud forest plants and animals are very useful to people. Some plants may give us new food crops. They have already given us medicines for cancer. Who knows what other discoveries will be made in the future?

Glossary

climate change   a long-term change in the weather conditions of an area

elfin   like an elf or elves

elfin forest   a forest that grows at the top of a mountain, with short, crooked trees

ferns   plants with long feathery leaves and no flowers

lowlands   low ground

mammals   animals with warm blood, like humans and cats and dogs, which have hair and usually give birth to live young

mosses   small plants without roots that grow in flat patches on trees, rocks, and damp ground

nocturnal   active during the night

orchids   plants with beautiful and unusual flowers

rainforest   a forest of tall trees that grows in a tropical area where there is a lot of rain

tropical cloud forests   forests in tropical areas that grow high in the mountains where trees are covered in clouds

Save the cloud forest!

Cloud forests are in danger from:

- **people cutting them down for wood**

- **animals released by man which damage plants and other animals**

- **climate change**

If we don't do something now, there may soon be none left!

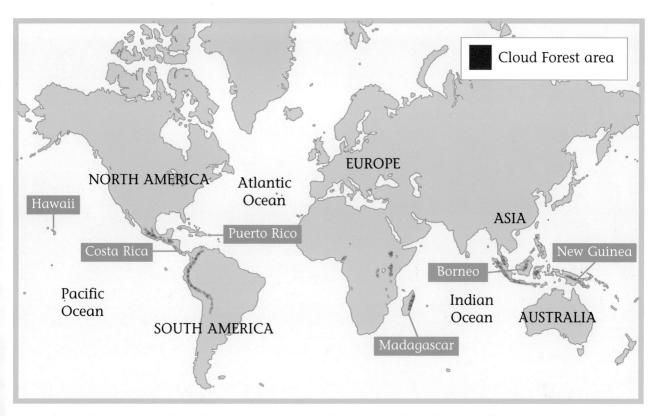

Cloud forests are found in many parts of the world and are still being discovered.

Why we need to save them:

- **Many of the world's rare and beautiful plants and animals live in the cloud forest.**

- **Cloud forests contain many secrets that may help people in the future.**

- **Cloud forests help stop flooding.**

- **Cloud forests collect water which helps people in lowland areas.**

Save the cloud forest ... before it's too late!

Ideas for guided reading

Learning objectives: locate information using contents and headings; read information passages and identify key points or gist; collect new words from reading; infer meaning from context; explain and present information, ensuring items are sequenced and details are included.

Curriculum links: Science – Plants and Animals, Variation; Geography – Passport to the World

Interest words: cloud forest, tropical, rainforest, elfin forest, Mount Kinabalu, Borneo, New Guinea, echidna, Vietnam, quetzal, gecko, Monteverde, Costa Rica

Word count: 1,295

Resources: whiteboard and pens

Getting started

This book may be read over two guided reading sessions.

- Ask the children what they know about forests, and the kinds of plants and animals found in them. Show them the front cover of the book and discuss what they think cloud forests are, checking the blurb on the back cover.

- Ask the children to skim through the book, and pick out interesting pictures and chapter headings.

- Read the first chapter (pp3–5) to the children and demonstrate how to summarise a fact from each paragraph, using a cloud-like fact map. Use facts from captions, as well as main text, for example beautiful flowers.

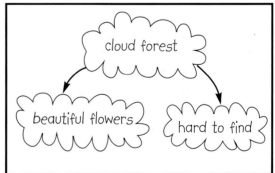

Reading and responding

- Ask the children to read silently and independently up to p29. Ask each child in turn to read a short passage aloud to you. Prompt and praise effective use of strategies for dealing with difficult and unknown words.